seasons of sacred lust

seasons of sacred lust:

THE SELECTED POEMS OF KAZUKO SHIRAISHI

Edited with an introduction by Kenneth Rexroth

Translated by Ikuko Atsumi, John Solt, Carol Tinker,
Yasuyo Morita, and Kenneth Rexroth

A NEW DIRECTIONS BOOK

© 1968, 1969, 1970 by Kazuko Shiraishi and Shichosha Publishing Co.
© 1970, 1975 by Kazuko Shiraishi and Sanrio Publishing Co.
Copyright © 1975, 1978 by New Directions Publishing Corporation

Some of these translations first appeared in *New Directions in Prose and Poetry.*

Manufactured in the United States of America
First published clothbound and as New Directions Paperbook 453 in 1978
Published simultaneously in Canada by McClelland & Stewart, Ltd.

Library of Congress Cataloging in Publication Data

Shiraishi, Kazuko.
    Seasons of sacred lust.
    (A New Directions Book)
    I. Title.
PL861.H57S413   1978   895.6'1'5   77-14936
ISBN 0-8112-0687-4
ISBN 0-8112-0678-5 pbk.

New Directions Books are published for James Laughlin
by New Directions Publishing Corporation,
333 Sixth Avenue, New York 10014

INTRODUCTION

Kazuko Shiraishi is certainly the outstanding poetic voice of her generation of disengagement in Japan. And there is certainly no woman poet of this kind anywhere near as good elsewhere in the world. Joyce Mansour in France is far inferior and Lenore Kandel in the United States equals her only in one or two poems. Her work has a fierceness and an exaltation that makes most of her Western colleagues in disaffiliation seem positively mellow. In the final analysis of course, what makes her preeminent is sheer poetic ability. If you hear her read aloud, with or without jazz accompaniment, you know that, even if you don't speak a word of Japanese, Shiraishi is the last and the youngest and one of the best of the generation of the Beats in America, the Angry Young Men in England, Vosnesensky in the U.S.S.R.

Shiraishi has often been compared to the novelist of extreme alienation Osamu Dazai or to Céline, but there is a most decided difference. Dazai and Céline were corrupted and eventually destroyed by their alienation. Shiraishi, like Henry Miller, is a remarkably clean liver. She doesn't take drugs, even alcohol, nor smoke either marijuana or the more dangerous tobacco. She stays up late, goes to discotheques and jazz clubs and loves to dance—hardly very vicious vices. Although sex enters into many of her poems and she has the reputation of being a very erotic poet, as a matter of fact her sexual life and attitudes differ little from those of any other liberated young woman in any of the major capitals of the world and it is very far from the random promiscuity of the hippie generation. Again, in this, she resembles Henry Miller. It's not just a moral difference. Shiraishi simply believes in keeping herself efficient as spokeswoman and diarist of what the French call the "métier." In this she resembles the great modern prose writer of the similar world of two generations ago, Nagai Kafu and Ihara Saikaku (1642–1693), the erotic writer of the métier of *genroku*—the brilliant period at the turn of the seventeenth to eighteenth centuries.

Similar, perhaps, but vastly changed. Kafu wrote of the last of the pleasure quarters of disintegrating Tokyo, the aging geisha and lonely prostitutes of seedy Shimbashi and the poorly paid actresses of the cheap theaters and satirical theater restaurants of Asakusa where he himself, even in old age, often acted. Saikaku wrote of a world of secular splendor.

Shiraishi's métier is something else. Modern Tokyo in the third quarter of the twentieth century is the international megalopolis pushed to the extreme. One cannot say to the ultimate, for God knows what the ultimate may be. Shiraishi does not write of the *ukiyo*, The Floating World, now utterly gone, but of a maelstrom, a typhoon, in which lost men and women whirl through toppling towers of neon. Shiraishi's Tokyo is straight out of Dante, but Paolo and Francesca seem only to get together for a moment to realize estrangement. Music—jazz and rock—and poetry provide something resembling values. Sex only seems to ease the pain and fear.

Poetry read to jazz had only a brief popularity in America. It was ruined by people who knew nothing about either jazz or poetry. Japanese, young and not so young, people have an astonishing musical knowledge of jazz and Shiraishi is certainly the best poet ever to use the form. Her poetry can be soft and sweet at times, but mostly it has a slashing rhythm read in what she refers to as her "Samurai movie voice." Her effect on audiences is spectacular. There is the secret of Shiraishi as a person and poet. She is a thoroughly efficient performer and her poetry projects as does that of very few other poets anywhere. Her peers are Dylan Thomas and Vosnesensky. She is also a woman of spectacular beauty.

Translation of Shiraishi presents very considerable problems. First, Japanese doesn't sound anything like American. A series of short lines beginning with "I" sounds nothing like the Japanese beginning "*watashi.*" Second, a translator must be hip, able to identify with this special world of Outsiders and familiar with their special languages in both Japanese and English. It's no job for squares or straights. This selection is the work of five people who constantly consulted one another. The principal initial translator of these poems was Ikuko Atsumi, a close friend of Shiraishi's, who herself writes poetry in both Japanese and English, assisted by John Solt of whom the same may be said. The translations were then revised by the American poet Carol Tinker, and by Yasuyo Morita and Kenneth Rexroth, who also translated several additional poems.

KENNETH REXROTH

FIREBALL—EGG OF FIRE

In a winter so cold that it hurt
When I put a rose on your table
It turned into an egg of fire,
And grew so angry
It was impossible for me to hold it
I let it be,
And it burned the table silently.
When I looked in the mirror,
My lipstick, necktie and everything else was on fire.
So I ran away from that house
With only a spoon in my hand.

NON STOP

There is a man who will never stop
Since he began to run.

As soon as he showed his head
Out of a window in a building,
He ran down the wall,
He ran down the road;
When the road ran out in the sea
He ran on the water.
I keep this man who runs on and on
And never stops
In my notebooks,
In my drawers,
In my darkness,
He forgets to let me sleep
But runs on and on.
And so my days are dead,
And my nights without end.

COLD MEAT

Am I off my head?
I sure am.
Is that a hat on your head?
My head is on my head.

In a chocolate shop,
Just between ourselves,
I want to talk about a pregnant cat.

You're not kidding, are you?
Of course not. I never kid.
I'm not kidding at all when I tell a lie.

So then give me some chocolate.
Please, kill it.
Even if it's dead, it is still itself.
Although I'm alive, myself is not myself anymore—
It will be the same, even as it grows cold.

STREET

It was when we walked on wet to our skins,
On a dark street in a miserable town.
Rain. Chilly weather.
We had raincoats and a black umbrella.
No matter how hard we waved to catch a cab,
They never stopped.
Finally we started to walk,
Wetly, tightly together,
And we wondered what future lay ahead of us.

Although I've never remembered anything
Of a warm hotel, of our bodies sharing their warmness,
Of our many words and acts of love.

FOOTBALL PLAYER

He's a football player
Kicks a ball, everyday he kicks a ball
One day
He kicked love up high in the sky
And it stayed there
Because it didn't come down
People thought it must be the sun
The moon or a new star

Inside me
A ball that never comes down
Hangs suspended in the sky
You can see it become flames
Become love
Becoming a star

FALLING EGG CITY

I rest on the edge of the green lettuce depth
While
The eggs come a-tumbling down—
Cheap ones, expensive ones,
From hardboiled eggs to boiling eggs,
And babies are falling down,
And rats are falling down,
And heroes, monkeys, and grasshoppers.
They are falling on the steeples and the playgrounds.
I tried to catch them with both hands,
But they slithered through my fingers
Like sorrow.
An absurd silk hat made a dramatic landing
On top of a skyscraper.
But the eggs kept right on falling
Into the cold veins of the vegetation.
What for?
(I don't know, don't know, don't know)
This is an editorial in the town newspaper.

POND

"Go home," I said,
"Tonight I don't want to be with you."
I said.
You went away sobbing,
"I don't have any home to go to."
Again and again
I traced your track as you went
From my heart, sobbing
Through the empty streets.
The stain of your tears
Soaked throughout my body
And formed a pond.
Beside that pond
Holding a heart heavier than ever
That night I went to bed.

HOLE

When your eyes and my eyes
Look into each other
At first we see a hole
Which belongs to you
And to me.
That's our hole
Which we produce and have never known.

Wondering if at first
There's a hole for us and next
If we have eyes to see it.
But already
Our brains hang down into the hole,
And our time begins to spread over it
Like a clock
In fact our wills are hung upside down.
They flap their legs and cry like birds
The words change to one costume after another
And the rope from sense to sense
Is cut off.

So our eyes regard each other
And blame each other because
There is a hole in the first place.

Who put a hand into the hole?
It is the hand that should be punished!

But
The numberless hands emerge from
Around the hole
And grow down thickly
Into its depths.

Opening my eyes and your eyes wide
Which possibly can't see
Why don't you listen as well to the new kinds of eyes
Which we don't know,
That are walking around?
Together, beside the hole.

IT WAS A WEIRD DAY

That day was weird.
Suddenly in April, the wind blowing,
Both of us, I and we, made it to "The Gym"
Checking out Sam & Dave
So Sam's song beats
Open and shut on
Them dancing there
Seen through the peephole.
Darkly down a dim hall,
An absentminded philosopher of good times
Sort of runs.
0.0.0.
Alone Sam reveals
His hard private swamp.

Eating cheeseburgers—
Let's have some coffee. It's cold.
Winter no more but so cold,
The wind grips with icy teeth.

That night we went dancing.
We made that club, this party.
"That man's got a forehead like a Volkswagen's ass"
"Oh, yeah, the company should pay him
A dead ringer"
Men excited women in tears
Someone gets ravenous.
Twin girls keep on dancing and won't stop.
At the crack of dawn everybody
Splits separately.
They all thought they'd each gone home
But maybe they had no place to go.
I split from us,
And came back to a weird place,
And conked out.

I FIRE AT THE FACE
OF THE COUNTRY WHERE I WAS BORN

I fire at the face
Of the country where I was born,
At the glazed forehead,
At the sea birds perched,
On that forehead—
Vancouver, beautiful city,
I shoot you because I love you.
Gasoline city, neither one thing nor another.
Neither
A prisoners' ward—without bars,
Nor the loneliness excreted
By lonely youth,
I wish it could be
a liberation ward,
a liberation ward, where petals of free thighs dance in the sky,
a freedom ward,
a happiness ward,
a goddamn it ward,
a goddamn it divine ward,
a profanation ward,
a devil's marriage ward,
a rich diet ward,
a senior citizen's lasciviousness ward,
a wanton woman ward,
a handsome boy ward,
a homosexual ward,
a wanderer's ward.
In the morning of this beautiful city,
With beautiful Lion Head Mountain
Covered with snow,
In the deep blue sky that soaks
Into the back of my eyes,

11

I find myself washing my face and teeth
In front of the wash bowl.
It's so sanitary—
A toothbrush and toothpaste kind of purity.
There is not a single bacterium in this country.
Not even that little tiny bacterium
Which the Devil called the soul can grow.
It doesn't exist.
All of them,
The King named Old Morality,
The people in power,
Who clothed the honest citizen
And named him Unseen Conservative,
Who stands at the bus stops—
One of them is a platinum blonde girl
Two of them are old women on pensions.
But nobody knows that the story
Of the beautiful girl who sleeps in the forest
Is about Vancouver.
No one knows that this beautiful city
Is the model for that beauty.
Victoria Vancouver, a girl,
A beautiful girl slowly coming towards me
Who opens her eyes but stays asleep
And comes to me smiling
A diplomatic smile.
I aim at the face of this country
Where I was born, and at the seabirds
Perched on the sleepwalker's forehead.
And then,
As the waves splash, moment by moment,
I stand ready to fire
With the pistol of confession.

A CHINESE ULYSSES

Turning back, he found no face,
No newborn face of his own.
Face is a country,
And his country was won away by red thoughts.
No longer with a face,
And with no lips to kiss,
He moves on.

His native land is under an unfamiliar map.
Only his mother's womb
Is the sign of a passport from his country of birth.
He fumbles for a name.
He left his country.
He is Ulysses
Who knows no return—
Ulysses barred from returning—
Ulysses who has no possible date of returning.
Holding wife, children, and flowers,
Burning a torch of poetry,
He cries toward the open sea,
"Is anybody there?"
Any faces proving he really exists?
A thousand, a million, a billion changing forms
Make love with the night sea and the stars falling on the waves
He enters their music
Seeking his interior country.
He joins the ascetics of lovemaking.
Though he can create thousands,
Tens of thousands, of his descendants' faces,
He'll never meet
Nor touch
The face of his newborn country.
So today,

Today again,
Ulysses
Crosses the sea and reaches land.
In a cold country town of Midwest America
He enters a building
At two in the afternoon.
Nobody
Pays any attention to him.
He is neither a personal attendant to the President,
Nor a gangster with a revolver,
Nor a muscle-bound world champion boxer.
He is tall and beautiful with a straight nose
And he carries a hidden dignity and fire,
But has no other characteristics.
So unless he is violent,
Or wears medals of honor,
People will just pass him by,
Because philosophy is an invisible living thing.
Nowadays people aren't scared of ghosts,
Especially living ghosts,
So he goes unnoticed for thousands of years.
He never dies.
He is not allowed to die.
He is Ulysses
A living myth.

"I feel wonderful today!"
He tells me while drunk.
But can he really feel drunk;
Can he get drunk in the sea of liquor
Listening to Sirens?
Would he know a Siren?
The Siren's voice changes to Elvis.
Is Presley a Siren?
Can a record from the rock 'n roll age
Carry him to Penelope?

14

He talks about a man who went to India,
A man named Snyder in search of self-realization.
He talks of the art of living freely.
He thinks of it as eating a rainbow,
As making love with a rainbow.
He hopes to grasp the far away clouds
And
The Siren
Goes to bed unfucked
Listening to Elvis's record.

He gets up in the morning,
Returns from lunch,
Is about to go to bed at night, and discovers
No face in the mirror nor in the bedroom.
Suddenly he realizes
He is Ulysses.
Still he can't go home
He can't go home
He has no country to return to—
Always moving on.

Blues
Reaches my ears
From the lonely country of a nameless man.
Beyond Dixieland jazz
It goes back thousands of years
To the first baby's first bath.

THE MAN ROOT

God if he exists
Or if he doesn't
Still has a sense of humor
Like a certain type of man

So this time
He brings a gigantic man root
To join the picnic
Above the end of the sky of my dreams
Meanwhile
I'm sorry
I didn't give Sumiko anything for her birthday
But now I wish I could at least
Set the seeds of that God given penis
In the thin, small, and very charming voice of Sumiko
On the end of the line

Sumiko, I'm so sorry
But the penis shooting up day by day
Flourishes in the heart of the cosmos
As rigid as a wrecked bus
So that if
You'd like to see
The beautiful sky with all its stars
Or just another man instead of this God given cock
A man speeding along a highway
With a hot girl
You'll have to hang
All the way out of the bus window
With your eyes peeled

16

It's spectacular when the cock
Starts nuzzling the edge of the cosmos
At this time
Dear Sumiko
The lonely way the stars of night shine
And the curious coldness of noon
Penetrates my gut
Seen whole
Or even if you refused to look
You'd go crazy
Because you can trace
The nameless, impersonal, and timeless penis
In the raucous atmosphere
Of the passers-by
That parade it in a portable shrine
In that stir of voices
You can hear an immensity of savage
Rebellion, the curses of
Heathen gism
Sometimes
God is in conference or out to lunch
It seems he's away
Absconding from debts or leaving his penis

So now
The cock abandoned by God
Trots along
Young and gay
And full of callow confidence
Amazingly like the shadow
Of a sophisticated smile

The penis bursting out of bounds
And beyond measure
Arrives here

17

Truly unique and entirely alone
Seen from whatever perspective
It's faceless and speechless
I would like to give you, Sumiko
Something like this for your birthday

When it envelopes your entire life
And you've become invisible even to yourself
Occasionally you'll turn into the will
Of exactly this penis
And wander
Ceaselessly

I want to catch in my arms
Forever
Someone like you

MY AMERICA

You've got me on the line
But baby I want to see you
America means my baby
Thinking won't help
It isn't politics on my mind
It's my baby
My darling darling America

So you're called America?
No, you're as nameless as your shining sweat
And you've got that barbecue bubbling up
With love
Delicious goo
So good in bed
I like the inside of your thigh
Your tough elegant penis
That doesn't let anything on
Wipes out the gods
O let me say my prayers
At a time like this

A kiss goodnight
After the late late show
Before bed
I get out either a kiss or a canned beer
I can't tell which comes first
In the morning you get up
To breakfast tasting
Like sun, shelf life, constraint,
And frigid freedoms—
Flavors that you spread around

You are pissed
Only when you blow it on the horses
Each trip to the market means
You draw another pool ticket
On Saturday night glued to TV
Dying to make an American million
Your bare teeth shining
Individualism
Egoism
Money lust
Optimism
All show in your face

          I can't hang out the wash
          It gets ripped off
          And this is hardly a slum
          Shut up!
          Open Nose is in the stretch
          He's third . . . he's third . . .
          He's third. . . . .

Off to North Dakota
So small a place
Smaller than Harajuku
A henhouse airport
The prop plane's oil stank up the sandwiches
Once down the ladder
Everyone suddenly focuses on me
And my old man

Snowflakes in the sky
Dance drier than sand
Noko laughs herself sick
Gil holds her tight
The lady rabbit that can't stop laughing
Under a wicked spell of kisses

20

I keep it tuned in three long days

The night train to Chicago
Let's take the A train
Lou Rawls's "Goin' to Chicago Blues"
We were so blue
As blue as tomorrow's blues
                    If you think about tomorrow
                    You gotta drink muddy water

Lou Rawls is always high
When he sings
In his hustler's threads on the street
So why does he sing "Stormy Monday"
On Friday
We got in on Friday
An eagle flew
Down at the womb station
Enormous, crummy, decrepit
Underground Mama had been waiting

Just say how often to loving
America baby
Nobody ever calls the American gentle anymore
They figure he's had it in Hollywood
Handsome, young, and loaded
Nevertheless heading over the hill
Suffering from three kinds of cancer
You only call hippies gentle these days

Homosexual love!
Stuff your pants
With chastity and some nice trade
And pass them to me
Special delivery to George's, Buggery Street
The roses go as soon as art

And are about as refined a taste
As cheesecake
Education, culture, art galleries, museums
Making kids strong and happy
Insure Madame Blanche's sound sleep

Baby, don't you cry
You've got to grow up big and strong
Dancing, holding,
Eating, fighting,
Making love, traveling,
Boxing, walking,
They cried in their sleep
The two of them pushed up the lid to love
But couldn't drink
You headed down the road of honey
How many more decades
America baby
Before
You baste with honey your infernal barbecue?

Hey stranger—
So you're called America?
You, glittering, nameless
My private custom-made America
Not processed, as fresh and sweet to me
As soul food
Spending a little time together
Soul time
Baby,
Keep your eye on the snake
But give me a kiss
Goodnight

MY TOKYO

I'm like Buddha
At last I've settled down on this town
October's knocked me up
With boredom

Nude my dearest friend
Hysterically vivacious
Paces a New York loft

You hang on Masuo's neck
And solicit kisses but
I just want to touch that thin
Coquettish body you've stripped from its frame
A dead white, the white chalk
Of a tough, empty ocean
That a flick of your finger flakes
Into dirty plaster pills
I see the thick pants of the Italian
Who hauls you off as laundry over his shoulder
Beer cans he bought us now roll empty
In the street floor bar
They squeal like rats
This is America, ravenous America

In Tokyo
My glum October
Hung over in sullen concrete
Aggravated by the phony tears of fake people
That jive around
Lipsalves streaming out of the jukebox
Are transformed into shoals of smelly sardines
That finally connect with ideas of poetry and art

Autumn, as always, holding classes
Kissing them all good-by
The time has come to retreat
Into my interior canal
I infiltrate my intimate city
And at the gate, at the end of summer
I score
Amenhotep, pharaoh of ancient Egypt
Once a young nobody
Nowadays a bus conductor
A butcher
A racing car driver
A poet
A revolutionary
And so on

All the rain
But not all
Old Egypt of five thousand years ago
A king
An eagle amulet
Guts of the newborn crocodile for bait
Pulpy brains of a baby
Unguents for rituals
Slinky dress of hatred
Time both the part and the whole
Holding hands with him, Amenhotep
Playing peekaboo in this chaos
We rushed into a season of personal appearances
Then
The noise of the subway
Rumbles through the pit of my womb city
On the stage drums and bass sounding
Sandra started her dance
Sandra, the Black dressed in black, never Salome

But a stunning lesbian, a nice middle class girl
A sweet, most dissolute mistress, a go-go dancer
She's a black madonna who turned her husband
Into a pale shark, a big star, a castrated Don Juan

Starting to take the subway
Led to my first meeting with Henry Miller
In the shit pot, newspapers, old letters
In chairs, in milk
In all the furnishings or food
I saw his drinking water, his microbes, his life of rags
I still ride the subway all the time
I've loved the subway for hours, as long as intercourse
The subway of my interior city's not made of iron
But of giving flesh
A ghost of civilization
A nest of thought
The most intimate gut of meditation
Migrants to my city
Between waking and sleep hang to the ulcer
Incessantly dribble
No words, no uproar, no pleas, no smiles
No seductions, no contentment, no bickering
Just bubbles

It's one in the morning at the Club "So What"
Max Roach beats his drum
Why does he look so good to me
I ask why his drumming is a lyrical accusation
His technique crowned by a rain of crushing sound
Numbs and enchants the audience
Inane spawners of eggs squashed flat
By the microcosm of his music

My Tokyo
The city that's almost a womb
Has got me standing at the gate
Making it with Amenhotep
And then the rain began
So long as we associated, dead or united
Five thousand years dead
Five thousand years born
Five thousand years of yawning
Five thousand years of laughs
To say that's love is underestimating
Everything
Frogs
Eggs
Jam
A piece of blue sky
Carbon paper
Records
And flies too
Let's dive between the sheets!
That's the password in this town
Someone went that way with a dead cat
Someone, too, and he was handsome
Crushed the mirror into shards
Clasped them to his penis and fainted
And somebody else
So timid of his delicate brain and body
Eating catnip
Cowered on the sheets wailing bitterly
These men embrace
Like two young leopards in the deep woods of their yearning
In each other's secret rooms
The ravishing monkey women
Balance rainbows of caresses like
The glow of morning

Then
My gig ran through October to November
It quickly bombed
Meanwhile I was tangled in the spider's web
Of sheer forgetfulness, sharp ecstasy, brooding manias
While
The spider got almost all of me
Captured with sloppy cries
One of me escaped
Made it to the subway and still
Tried to make some sort of music
This may not be love
Merely the greetings of the season
But
At least something was committed to music
I'm smeared with the new melody
And hear my tail thrashing as furiously as a crocodile of hatred

But who gets slapped
Who is this ghost ordered into music
O
I sight Joe as a ghost at the terminal
He's been crushed beneath the sexual roller
And has become a gray shadow
He's magnetic sand expelled into the spermless desert
Forsaken by the last drop of his accumulated life
And wound in the coils of a viper
Is borne slowly by the spider
Far from the limb of his will
And rusted fast in the side of delayed time
He is going to lower the last curtain

If I'm poking hard
The hot will in the ashes
It's so I can bury my city completely

Forced through a fog of foreboding
I could barely hear God's pain
Then it reached agony
Now for the first time I behold
God entire, falling in a thunderbolt, roaring
And landing hot at my side
This vision is momentary and aeons long
Lying half suffering, half wounded
Masqueraded like an exhausted pilgrim

My city is
Now far distant
It snuggles close to the stranger's face
It's head drooping on its concrete neck

A PURRING LION

Yesterday, because I was a lion
I was purring a tune in the jungle
As all the stars began to fall
All together.
And my body was burnt all over
Every time I trod on the moonlight.
And the skin was scraped
From the tip of my nose
And my life was charred with love.
My mane gave itself to the wind
And left with no idea of where to go—
To the past, to the future, or to death
Nor will my tail and ears ever come back to me.

Today on my way from school
I walked straight through the front of the mirror shop.
That's why I remember nothing but this:
Because I left my tweezers in the jungle,
I will never be able to recover
Anything but the words of my purring.

TIGER

All day long
A tiger kept coming in and out.
The room was falling into ruin and
Broken arms, legs, and chairs were
Crying at the sky.
Even though the tiger has not come all day,
There was no certain place to put each of
The broken arms, legs and chairs.
They had lost their places.
They howled like milk and wind.
They went on howling
Creaking against the sky.

FLEA

I am a bloodsucker.
I am the world's number one son of a bitch.
I take revenge for hopeless love.
A beautiful girl is irritated,
Makes a face, pouts, scratches
And finds me.
So I decide to kill her.
I deliberately reach out
My sharp polished nails to her.
Then my pleasure begins to come.
Keeping out of sight at the risk of my life,
I suck her blood and run away.
I am a sadistic flea.

MONKEYS

"It doesn't matter that we will never become human beings.
It doesn't matter that we still have tails.
We don't care if we never
Become God or Philosophy.
It's enough that we love each other."
Said the monkeys as they shimmied and danced
And talked of love in tail language,
Like deaf and dumb language.
On the other hand,
Male and female human beings today
Are always saying,
"We can't find love.
We can't believe in it."
That's because they don't have any tails,
So their empty souls wander
In a fog of insincerity.

GORILLA

I never dreamed Jiji the gorilla would fall
In love with me.
I used to like Jiji.
Though he was ugly,
His heart was pure,
So very singlehearted and faithful,
So very gentle and yet so violent.
The reason I liked Jiji so much
Was we were just friends.
As soon as he opened his heart to me
I suddenly showed him a heart of stone.
Oh, Jiji
I'm sure I am a wicked and hateful bitch.
I suddenly hated Jiji
So much I wanted to tear him
To pieces and barbecue him.
Oh my gorilla! Jiji!
You are a real human being.
I am a false beast who has sold my soul to the devil—
What else could I be?

PARROT

I said, "I love you."
You answered, "I love you."
I said, "I hate you."
You answered, "I hate you."
I said, "Shall we separate now?"
You answered, "Shall we separate now?"
Always, always,
You were a parrot.
It was all because you repeated my words exactly
That we came to separate.

RHINO

That man is a rhinoceros-oyster.
He is so big and strong,
But with a heart like a delicate petal.
Don't be cold to him.
Don't fall in love with him for fun!
If you love him seriously
You will know that
Nothing could be more fearful
Than his love, a love of an oyster-rhino.
If he ever discovers
You are unfaithful, Carmen,
He will take you down the road to death
On his horn,
Instead of kissing you with his gentle eyes.
Don José is a rhino-oyster.

SHEEP

Have you seen Utamaro's pictures?
I remember a man
Quietly watching a woman combing her beautiful hair.
The woman was watching the man.
Their eyes were gentle, yet intense and vehement as fire.
One day, suddenly a ewe in a zoo showed me
The same gentle fire-eyes as the woman's
In Utamaro's picture.
No one listens to the music called love,
No one knows it at all,
But I saw it for a moment
In the expressionless eyes of a ewe in a zoo.

ANTELOPE

A girl with legs like an antelope,
A boy with legs like an antelope,
Fell in love and got married
And had a pretty child
With legs like an antelope.
The child's father went away.
Where?
If you track the fast legs of an antelope
You need a faster heart.
Unfortunately in this world
There are very few hearts
As farsighted as
Antelope legs.

DOG AND MAN

There is a dog in the back yard
Crying, "I'm hungry."
And a man at the front door
Crying, "I want to see you very much."
"I want love."
"I'm so sad."
A man cries at the front door.
A dog cries in the back yard.
Man or dog,
Who is more sad,
Hungry, or lovelost?
Who is more bitter?
God!
What is the answer?

ALLEY RAT

I am a city rat.
I trick the pigs
And scurry up an alley.
I am an evil player.
This rat has kept off starvation
As a thief as long as he can remember.
I am a thief of love, food, money, passion.
I am suspicious of everybody
In the back alleys of the city.
"Kick this stud out!"
But who can kick out the
Dark night in a rat's eyes?

SUGAR BABY BEAR

Honey, strawberries, cake,
Sweet wine, peaches, candy too—
Sugar Baby Bear has to have his sweets all the time.
And that means even music, clothes, voices, love.
"If it ain't sweet, it ain't for me.
Everything's got to be just as sweet as sugar."
So here's this sweet man,
Doing sweet things, and
Living just as sweet as
A honey-licking bear,
This man here with his sleepy honey eyes,
With his pretty face.
But he's got a body exactly like a bear—
Hey, can't you see the fur
Spread over
His great big chest?

PANTHER

You are so optimistic, young and realistic.
You are not a king at all,
But a bright, cunning and agile panther.
After jerking an antelope
Up into a thorn tree,
You eat lunch,
Precisely, carefully, cleanly,
With etiquette and ethics of a panther—
Ladies and gentlemen!

DEDICATED TO THE LATE JOHN COLTRANE

Suddenly
He went to heaven
John Coltrane

In several ways
You were drastic about living
Out of your beauty
Beyond any meaning
A blue rain began to fall
People
Sit cross-legged on the richness of meaning
And like beggars grab the rice of sound
Eating, they weep goldly
Uncontrollably in misery

Coltrane
You have entered through
A hole in heaven

Because you died
On earth, again, one huge
Soundless hole has opened
People
Crawl to the edge of that pit
Missing him and his sounds
They clutch his thrown away shirts
Or album covers
Yearning sadly, loving him
They groan, get angry, and cry

Kulu Sé Mama
Kulu Sé Mama

Coltrane
With your extremely heavy
And short pilgrimage
Full of fleeting eternity
Spirit traveling
You were mainly blowing thoughts
Thoughts are eyes, wind
Cascades of spicy sweat
Streaming down your forehead
Thought is an otter's scream
The sexual legs of chickens
Killed by your old lady
Boiling in a pot
Women's pubic hair
Alice or Aisha
Thoughts are the faceless songs
Of pink stars
Squirming in the sky
Of every woman's womb

Hot, dark summer afternoon
Coltrane
Your 'Olé'
So full of romanticism and power
Now we don't have your 'Olé' of love
For a little while, about as long as forever,
We won't receive your
"*Olé*"

On this earth
In this human hot arena
In the bullring
Cicadas are crying now
Hot, dark summer
Sits by itself
No bulls, no glory

Only shadows and memory
You in my memory
Coltrane, your music

People see the colors of your sounds
So passionately
They listen with ears of dread
To the ordeal of your sounds

For forty-one years
In your very busy history
The sun often rose and sank
Orange sun, African sun, American sun
The taste of human sun
Rose and set hundreds and thousands of times
In a black, soul room
You are sunbathing
That dude the sun shines brightly
On your silent back
That dude the sun often cried
And became the sweat of blinding music
Diving into a saxophone blown by you
He cried out loud and free

Brilliant blue
Even the orange sun
Against those black, desperate cheeks
Has begun to cry incoherently
Coltrane almost became a sky
He became a cascade of will
Carrying the sounds
He made them fall
Pouring them out

We know the monsoon
In John's long lasting solo
The blazing rain continues

We are often beaten with the rainfall of sound
We are numbed
To the deepest room of our hearts
We are soaked through
The door breaks, the mast snaps
The chairs float away
Then we regain that certain consciousness

Which is volition
Which is desire
It is the cosmos announcing
The trivial existence of humans
Alone, carrying his saxophone
He takes giant steps
Walking through the cosmos
Though his stride helps us see the blue
Unstable vertebrae of earth
His expression was mostly invisible
Sometimes he mysteriously, shyly
Buried his face in a cloud

John, wandering Coltrane
Even though you are no longer on earth
I, we remember you when you were
All of a sudden
We recall you wandering for awhile
In the season without answers
With your face hidden
In that opaque cloud

While flowing slowly down the river of agony
You met the fish of pleasure
You met love
You met woman, son, friend, God
You met music and its Holy Spirit
Then you became the Holy Spirit
You became the music itself

On earth, from now on
A long, hot, dark summer continues
Even though you died
Even though your transient life ended

On earth
In whatever cold struggle
Hot passions and determinations
Are smoldering
Humans are walking on the day

John Coltrane
Your day, that day which was once alive
That day which met 'someday'
That day which dissolved the next moment

Coltrane
In the way I love you
I love the days you lived through
I love the season of those days
Which you survived for forty-one years
You music, your voice
Your glory and rage
Your love and conviction
Your God, your Holy Spirit
Your cosmos with East and West
Its desperation and grief

All those I love and warm
And meditate upon
May your spirit rest in peace
Our beloved John Coltrane
A tremendous saxophone player

For the strong, black soul
Of Saint Coltrane
In heaven

SEASONS OF THE SACRED SEX MANIAC

Winter

When December comes
Instead of winter it's
The season of sacred lust
Autumn used to be
But then winter didn't come so easily
Illegitimate children of sacred lust
Became lovely and pitiful monkeys
And while they danced around the Christmas tree
Hand in hand joyfully in a circle
At last the sacred winter of the sex maniac
Arrived

These days
The earth stopped cooling itself as before
The North Pole increased its soft tears year after year
And on the dirty backs of penguins
Who had once been the favorite mistresses of this secret room
The Borgian poison called city
Smeared itself

Once in spring on a shallow day
And then on a summer evening
A monkey entered the house from the balcony
Seeking fleas
The monkey spent three years nursing
At a woman's breast
He's three hundred years old now
And the woman is already three thousand
But she receives hot dark signals from the stars' pupils
Not three thousand but thirty million years away
Gravitation of darkness which winks out of the cosmic cellar

Brutality of insignificant sublime romance
For which a woman blows
A blue sounding whistle
Towards the woods of transcendence
She whistles beyond transcendence
To a magnetic storm of love

Turning back
I found February standing around Pisces
With dimples on both cheeks
As he is a basketball player
He jumped as high as he could
And threw some round thing from his arms
Into a basket
The basket is
Somewhere in the universe
But no one knows
Whether in the Milky Way or the golden
They think he's a winner
But he's alone, oiling
A moderately sunburnt woman's back
On a towel inside a hot summer beach house
He smokes leaves
You can find the leaves at the foot of the mountain
When you go driving
You'd better pass the policeman cautiously
February has gone by Pisces now
And meditates on some stardust
Thrown on the American West Coast
March is nowhere
He met nobody
But April certainly found itself
As Muhammed Ali with the number 5 on his back
During April Fool's Day
He introduces his little grayhaired parents to everybody

He went into a hotel beauty salon
And touched someone's face buried in a white cloth
Doesn't the face look like a flower?
But there are some very ugly flowers
Whenever he caught sight of his rival Foster's face
Ali vomited
He was suffering from morning sickness at the sight
    of his face

In May frogs croak in the rice fields
Cleopatra every night
Was attacked in her tent
By boys on whose heads
Tomatoes were planted
They threw mad tomatoes at her
Waiting for her to die of old age
Or to fall victim to dysentery
With mad tomatoes, but
She managed to stay alive
And crept little by little
Towards June or July
Borrowing the sideways crawl of a crab
For her dance routine

A black motorcycle runs
Tearing an August night right in two with its sound
The black motorcycle that runs up some raw flesh
Which is nobody
But myself
I'm a high holy master of the occult
A lewd detective that
Has mastered the art of self-division
From 2 to 4, 4 to 8
I skillfully slip from the raw flesh
Into September's "Misty"
At the club "Mingus' Music"

50

Jonnie Hartman, ending the interview
Lays his cigarette on the table
And begins to sing "Misty"
The ears of the people in the club's darkness
Become flapping bats
They were covered with goose bumps though it wasn't winter
In October Captain Cook is no longer a captain
He sails on the sea of saxophone notes
But in such a violent storm of sound
Even though an expert
He has no confidence in the future
Whether he sights land to starboard or a dinosaur
He just proceeds
This Cook Junior, though no longer a captain
Just proceeds on over the sea
Where the future declines by degrees into darkness

When I fly a kite
In November
I find a boy flying in the sky
Sometimes you see in a field
A boy flying
And a kite flying the boy
At that moment on earth
On a rare green road
Which is very rare these days
A young beggar walks along
He's skinny, crooked, long-legged
A young monk, a hungry monk who knows no religion, no love
Putting a black radish of lanky ego-sutra between his thighs
He hangs out his solitude with clothespins
At the corner of the universe
He believes this is purity and
Lets half his face show in the blue sky
Only half his face timidly
Appears in the blue sky

Everybody suddenly imitates Mary
All the men and women pretend to conceive
Trying to start a profane Christmas
Here and there on earth
Monkeys' first tender cries and
The cries of mothers in childbirth
Obscenely ring out together
Everything at last seems
To make a circle
We hear the sound of a flea jumping
From hundreds of years away
Sacred lust
That is an autumn stud horse
Celebrating the holy winter of the sex maniac
Celebrating Christmas
Lovely monkeys
Pitiful monkeys
Monkeys of joy
Gather in a hall
To dance in a ring
Around the fir tree of December

When we dance in a ring
Around the fir tree of December
The year
Instantly
Becomes a cardinal
The cardinal as James Brown
His sweet cold sweat
Man or woman?
Anyway he's the world
James Brown
The cardinal of sex in the holy land
The holy land where monkeys
Swarming in a hall
Appear and disappear in these sacred seasons of lust

52

I also want to be with you
Male and female monkeys
Screaming over and over
Draw closer to him
Boiling all over his sexy voice
So as to be beaten by his hot Niagara Falls of madness

This cardinal is afflicted with a rare disease
And all alone while counting
The Mona Lisa's pubic hair
He recalls the ancient mother of penis
Slices it and is sliced
Neither people nor monkeys
Can kiss affectionately
The Buddha's merciful solitude
Shines brightly in the gold and vermilion cape
Of the cardinal
His wild and sorrowful flesh
Flesh that starts to rot tears itself madly
Dancing and barking away
They only shed tears
At a distance
Snakes coil around their feet
From their feet towards me
Or towards the center of your universe
Snakes creep up
And try to smother constellations
Especially the two tails of Pisces
But there's a huge hollow horse neck without eyes
Staring at Pisces
The horse neck star
Always strives for a good view
With large, rocky, eyeless eyes
Stretching his neck to see
The clever snakes get it
Grinding his agile waist he climaxes

From junk ornaments
A beauty like a fat white cow
Emerges shaking tens of thousands of years
Thrusting water aside
Dressed in nothing but a veil of mist
This beauty aged ten thousands of years
Isn't going anywhere
But is heading straight
Into the black hole
The Swan's black hole beyond tens of thousands of light years
So that she'll be absorbed after a long, transient sleep
When everyone wakes up
He sees right away
The black hole
Of the cosmos
Or of himself
James Brown
The chasm of his voice
Into the black hole at the depth of the chasm of his voice
Thousands, tens of thousands, or hundreds of millions of souls
Are being absorbed, tied in a row
For a few seconds
While he shifts from Mona to Lisa
All the just born babies
All the long lived people whose faces are drowning
        in their wrinkles
Women like men, men like women
Men like men, women like women
All the human beings like cows, monkeys
Lambs and tomatoes
In an instant
Turn into flames
And absorbed into the black hole
In midwinter
Of Cardinal James Brown

Are the flames
In the cardinal's darkness
Or are they inside the ones absorbed?
Anyway
Here is the monstrous parade of flames
Of the figures of those who've fallen into
The black hole of this singing man's throat
With voices cackling in agony
The sacred sex maniac is hardly ever
Contented by stillness but
Gradually walks
To the spring ridge of the active volcano
In each step bathed by the ejaculation of light. . . .

At the end of this earth
In the midst of the cosmic park
The bird star chirps
Everything else is still
On the other hand
Our transient cardinal
James Brown already dead
Continues living at the back of his corpse
Taking a rest he smokes temporary love

Pretending to rest
He listens alone
To the incessant soundless music of eternity
Which his own black hole plays

Spring

I was well into April, season of the sacred sex maniac
When I saw at the western edge of the Pacific
The face of God, full of failure, diving into the sea
Directly down in front
He dropped his voice
On the bad connection
On the point of leaving
For eternity
Eternity, that is,
Extinction

I saw terrifying young love
Between the thighs of an antelope
In the furious sigh
Of the earth's heated dirt
That forces horsetails I saw
The pregnant soil
A man is there who drills a well of spirit
A tattooer
Who for long months and years
Continuously dug and stabbed the spirit's depths

He's ignorant of the fragrant destiny of his tattoo
The crooked and cruel exhilaration of his fate
But he's still the tattooer
Who ultimately becomes a tattoo
Of a rose named man
Deeply penetrates this woman's soul
And turns into an eternally sleeping picture that never wakes
So that each time the soul of the woman swings
The rose tattoo laughs darkly in his voice
Shedding tears of blood

The earthworm calling
Or a robin singing
So the natural voice of the season calls out
Outside the woman, but
She's the tattooed lady
She's a dark room impervious to ruin
The woman is the dark room
In the dark and bewildered world
Where daybreak will never come
The woman says to herself
Maybe, she says,
Maybe this might last for some kind of eternity

I was not so afraid of dying
But parting was. . . .

A man too much alone
Lived terribly long and fast
For five years
At the end when the five years
Suddenly turned transparent and melted
His ex-woman
His goddess is singed and sore from burning in lewdness
The sunset colored weekend is caught in a spider web
She seems no longer a goddess but instead a spider
Then again a goddess
The man squatted, sneezed and blew his nose
In a peculiar place
Crumpling the world into a ball
He wiped his face with it
The crumpled world stuck to his face

He could stand in the world bluntly
Like a map
But never allowed to caress the world

Man is
Man is almost a dog
Thinking that way makes him almost man
Almost sorrow and despair
And the world is whole
What does it mean?

Let's go bowling now
Let's quarrel and watch boxing now
Let's go now
Just drop in on life
On your way to the graveyard
Let's go let's go
On the streetcar, images, suffering
Reality and so on
Scorning the scenery in which a love gourd sways
Hating, loving, falling in love. . . .

A week went by
But yesterday was already in eternity
Hundreds and thousands of days
That have never returned became smoke over there
Sometimes I heard the smoke turning into fire
And sobbing
Hot tears of hell
Streaming slowly away through the thighs
Toward our ancestors' spirits
Humming
Turned into a rainbow

Yesterday I cut down
Old time and memory
Kicked them over the cliff
And slept holding a new tree
The tree had no name nor memory
It was just like
A young man

Sweet wines proclaim unanimously
Being lewd is nothing but loving
A son of a bitch runs in tennis shoes
At the end of spring, not in the West but in the East
The women of the race
For a moment transformed into rabbits
Got excited by the beautiful bandy legs
Of that race called son of a bitch
And in spite of themselves wept, their mouths dropping open
At the senseless pure belief
Of the son of a bitch's crystal eyes

The cherry blossoms bloom, it's Easter
Nothing but the Resurrection could be hell
We've got Resurrection, we've got hell
I can't believe everything lasts, never perishing
Constantly born, continuously living, writhing in agony
And at last even resurrects . . . .

The Eternity Man can never leave
His eternity
He tries all the time to get to sleep
But the devil's serious love
And God's unsympathetic tenderness
Wake him who is falling asleep in life

I was in East Asia
Holding anemones in my arms
I was about to go and hand
This tiny bouquet
To a traveler in the spring of life
I also bought a transparent umbrella
And a raincoat more transparent
I made my body which would never be transparent
Get into it
I loved the naked body of woman

Like a sower
Who makes sorrow and beauty bloom
Like an anemone on every part of a woman's body

Sam the sower didn't know how to make it bloom
But he was a beautiful wounded panther
Who knew how to howl
He scattered like beads
Love's pain inlaid with spirit
On every corner of his black skin

Sam chewing time up well, served his lover well
His lover ate and licked
His gift of time greedily like a beggar
He bent her far back over his skin
Wanting to lap up the last drop of juice
Going "around the world"
His lover, gloating, gobbles on

My ordinaries have started
At night the man is going to fill my stomach
With barbecued bird
And put my unhappiness to rest for a moment
In the bathtub of love
And also taking with him the seeds of dark angels
He is to guide me from hell
Slowly to heaven
So childish but so sincere
This proper, upright soul gets on my nerves
Unhappiness detests perfection
Because it's superior
And nobody wants to be happy
But waits around to be unlucky
Man is bored to death
With being so human

Man wants to be a wolf
Wants to be locoweed
A son of a bitch
He wants to ruin himself
As a victim of the son of a bitch's moods
The male and the female fuck, a drama
Which they immediately want to wreck

All rush toward death
They long to go and die
They almost
Want children
And then they're sorry
Miserable about aging
They are dying to age rapidly
Human beings don't want eternity
They want annihilation
They don't want to be a life
But a romance
They'd rather be a rose
A worm
And to be squashed like a worm
Eternity is a harsh rose
It is a harsh penalty

So I send him into
Eternity
Day by day
O momentary
Moments!
And young trees and subways
Actions, silences
Heavy set, honest love!
O tenacious penises!
Prides, young men's eyes
Waterfalls of tears splashing down the abyss!

Live fish of love and anger
Sam X
You, one of the nameless
I won't make you eternity
You are presence
You are love that will perish
The jealous, tenacious and momentary dark side
You are a revenge, a struggle, a single obsession

And besides
You who are human!
I'll love your cock
As much as your soul
I'll love the sensitive beat of your heart
As much as the spring of your muscles
I'll love your innocent happiness
As much as your childish unhappiness
Your tender faith
As much as your fierce betrayal
Your slave's modesty
As much as your cruel monarchy
The strong jab of your boxing
As much as the refreshing sound of your trumpet
Your angel's indifference
As much as your devil's fascination

When I sleep with man
Ten years go by in a hurry
Man is sleep
Sex is a medicine, dope,
And love is hatred, a skeleton
Love that hangs down from the tip of jealousy
Is a counterweight to the universe
Which makes me rush at last
To the awakening

His April ran wild
After cherry blossoms fluttered down
Suddenly sleet fell
He tried to turn back as far as winter
Or suddenly mounting the season
Tried to push on to tomorrow

April, the son of a bitch
Cruel, sweet, sentimental
Because it's almost love without responsibility
And it's momentary
It's almost eternity
During this time
One or two went on a trip
A letter came
From June in Oklahoma
Saying, "I've given up on Whitey."

Parting is always sentimental
Memories almost inevitably give out steam
June, you romantic!
The dog is darling
Because in his sorrow
He honestly shudders

I came and went between the days
I made a round trip many times a day
Between things to build and things to destroy
I gradually came to know
That I would build something
So cursing God
I loved the child of the crab that turned into the Devil
But we can't be crabs
Crawling doesn't begin anything
He quickly mastered
Beautiful forms of karate
Is it a line beautiful for building
Is it building that points to the ultimate destruction?

The sleet let up
In April there was some fine weather
When I view April from the outside
Though it might not be what he had in mind
April seemed to recover
His usual good humor
Then I went to see a woman who is making a white snake
Bearing pansies and chocolate
In my silver outfit

Men are passing shadows
Is shadow truth or fiction?
In any case
Men are shadows
That live and flit by

A young shadow that will soon flit by
Now drifts over my tracks
Just missed by the thunder of a rainbow

The season of the first snow
When the headache of love begins
Slowly begins to fall
In his brain

A life that flashes by!
Forbidden feet hurrying!
He who is about to vanish
Lands on the spot where he ceases to exist
Who was trapped
Over the ocean of time?
Inside the pure pitch black character of smooth fur
At his pure white time
The moon rises
Death in desolation
Cuddling closer than all the dead
Sucks up silence

Death is not sweet
But poetry is sweet
Your life is not sweet
But your being
The scenery where your soul's rain falls
Is sweet
I am not sweet
But we are
For we are a resolve
A romantic resolve
Human beings named will
Well then
The unseen American dream
That carries our resolve
Is not sweet
America's dream
Arranges that the living and the dead
Total the same
Wonderful
Should indicate surprise
As well as splendor
I conceive you here
We bugger each other here
I curse you, cultivate you, and pray
Performing the secret ritual of caress
Here
Taking the streetcar tonight
We'll meet and we'll make love
You are nameless
Even if you're not
So what

You yourself are lonely
Fluttering in namelessness, the sea of all existence
Nobody except you

A single resolve is always cruel

My dear
I am starting to write a very long letter
I can't see it
Nor can you
We start to write a very long letter
Start to walk on a very long resolve
We start to write a very long letter
But this "long" doesn't mean eternity
It is the stretch of human beings
As long as they live
As long as their resolve is moist
It is the stretch of man
Not of eternity
I
And we
Start to write
A very long letter
Not to eternity
But to a
Long stretch
Today

Autumn

In the fall the monkeys howl
A monkey, yearning for a human
Leaves the balcony
Enters a woman's breast
Becoming a nursing child
While searching the monkey for fleas
The woman gradually turns into autumn

Soon she will be winter
But before she becomes winter
A man severs sexual duty with a Japanese sword
A naked man who cut off his penis
Heads this way through windy Musashi field
He thinks it's fine to head over here
But he cannot comprehend what here means
A boy with a flame fingered badge
On the back of a blue jumper
Announces
I want to be a homosexual
From his front door
The boy peeped at a girl's privates
From there he entered the girl's cellar
Passing up through the gulf of the stomach
To her throat
He asked around
He spent three years
Until he got bored with only a front view of the naked
A hairy monster signals to him from the American base
     at Yokosuka
And when he squats in the eerie pampas field
Stealthily waiting for
The monster's attack
A fox yelps
The moon rises
And the boy finds himself playing tag alone

Dying by chopping off his head
Or dying by chopping off his cock
It's death still the same
Says the woman riding a horse
Her hair upended in annoyance
She bitches that her old man
Died without leaving a will

While whipping her horse
She goes on through Musashi field
That sets your teeth on edge
The purple field with hallelujah skies
Where a golden sunset glows

Poetry! Jazz!
Men who force sound from their throats
Men and women
Ripping and scattering words from their bowels
Gather in a damp, cold attic in Shinjuku
The whiskers of city rats are long
The head hair and pubic hair of city men are long
While nobody notices a rat gnaws
A long thin cock lying on the floor
A putrid sausage
For a glass of water
For a glass of music
For a glass of words
Long haired tribes
Gather here
In a dark, damp attic in Shinjuku
So then will their hunger be satisfied?
No, their hunger will be all the more absolute
They've come to OK their hunger
Nobody admits he's lonely
They all think loneliness is a pipe dream
Not their daily bread
Bread isn't loneliness
Eating isn't loneliness
But when bread, eating and I
Exist
Loneliness spontaneously
Begins to masturbate

The moon rises
What moon?
A crescent moon
Or a very full white moon?
No. A moon must be
Red, bloodstained,
Sort of gloomy and big
And shaped like a head
That enters the asshole
When I see the moon
Especially the red moon
It reminds me of a girl
Who has never held the red moon close
Since birth only purplish black moons
Have given her assistance
So she came to the city
Came to sing
In high heels
In a metallic black dress
What is Sophistication?
Something like noodles?
Tears made of noodle silk?
Sacred sperm of noodles?
Noodles are tears falling in sheets
From Christ's eyes
And Christ's sacred seed

When winter comes it's Christmastime
But there aren't any stables these days
And no straw beds for the birth of man
Man doesn't give birth to man
But to cockroaches
Cockroaches just like us
Get together to have a party
Merry (What is merry?)
Anyway, Merry Christmas!

But the snow doesn't fall
The man who was about to die
Choked on candy on New Year's Day
And vanished
Instead the monkey hunts a tender little flea
On the breast of the woman who has become the New Year
The flea is tenderness sucking blood
Which is more threatening,
Tenderness sucking love or tenderness sucking blood?
The boy says
My mother turned into white blood and died
When I was five
My young mother died of leukemia
Then three days later my father. . . .
That's the end of the story
Young mother and father, hand in hand,
Have gone on the journey to heaven on a train delayed
    three days
White blood is the ticket to heaven
Tenderness sucking blood
What follows is
Tenderness sucking love

Dietrich
Who reaches forty on her birthday
Keeps black goldfish at Nishiogi
Ginsberg's dead mother Naomi
Shows herself at the banquet
Masked like a ghost, riding in a limousine
Tetsuo Nakagami chants poetry sutras
Yoshiaki Fujikawa and the Now Music Ensemble raise jazz
    To Nishiogi of the whole world
    To Shinjuku of the whole world
    To Ushihama of the whole world
This chanting of poetry and jazz united
Excites the horny ghosts in heaven

And even drunk ghosts on earth
Become hot and stiff
Even cocks without pussies have tentative erections

On the other hand
Dietrich
Won't be forty
Doesn't keep black goldfish
Dietrich is a nun
An incarnation of Mari Ibuki
The ex-stripteaser, the queen
On her sexy nun's robe
A shower of cherry blossoms
Fall in warm heaps of snow
They melt into wine
Horsetails bloom,
But Nun Mari
Won't shake her ass in a horsetail dance anymore
This spring she lives for the mass of the dead horsetail
Living doesn't mean living
Living is dying
The petal's storm is sharp, living to die

In the splendor of spring
The Spring Man's cock stretches and stretches on and on
Jack's the Spring Man and his penis the bean stalk
A giant man climbs the bean stalk
But on the Spring Man's penis
No giant falls asleep after gorging
No Jack runs up this bean stalk
Tell me how could the Spring Man
Climb his own cock?

There is a legend in Fussa town
That when a sixty-year-old lady
Plays the shakuhachi

Ripping up roses
All the snakes, white and black
Young and old, gather and
Line up
For each snake the shakuhachi music costs 2,000 yen
The old lady's an angel as ugly as sin
There are no tender devils, only the ugly angel's tongue
The angel is an evil
Superior to the gourmet devils
Because so long as the devil is enticed
By tasting the feeling of going to heaven
He cannot pull the angel down

A marvelous, hot summer!
Jim sweating at basketball
Two white pig men of civilization
Go away happy, drooling at the mouth
Their heads between women's thighs
So it's sweet little Jennifer
Hardly born, splitting her mother red
Chocolate, such pretty eyelashes, she takes after
    her mother—
But
Summer in a second
Got herself off on a typhoon, then miscarried

Men and women
Have lost summer
Tomorrow's exclusive prediction: earthquakes
Too many people
Too many cars
People produce words, use them, it's time to
Get rid of the garbage

All mount like huge columns of cloud
Nothing ever shrinks
In the mounting wrong
In spite of that
A man with sexy eyes gets in a plane
Because he's a pilot
And like a horsefly
Whizzes around the round head of this earth
Each time he flies
The air suffers more from asthma
El, the dog at Saitama
Guards black chickens
A full grown person
Gets down to gobble red strawberries
While El the dog
Looks after black chickens

When autumn comes
Chickens have turned into cocks
But El the dog still guards
Black chickens
No longer eating strawberries
The person is about to turn into them
The person is willing to become red blood
Though he wants to be eaten
The person can't eat
Or be eaten
However
El the dog
Still looks after black chickens

ONCE AGAIN, THE SEASON OF THE SACRED LECHER

Pitch-dark
In the pitch-dark depths of the universe
A silver wave runs, a fish, an electric wave,
A determination runs

Sound of waves lapping, gradually coming closer
Silver River,* in the wave lapping Silver River
A hunter fishes for beauty
Our guardian deity
The sacred lecher appears

Grace's amber cheeks
Universe
From the pitch-dark depths suddenly
The Silver River stars fall
Onto a close-up of Grace's
High cheekbones
On Grace's amber cheeks
The universe now flows
Silver waves overflow
Dark-red and rose lamé fish cross-fly

For a moment earth stops
On the cheeks of Grace, the model,
And opening its eyelids
Turns a magnet toward the unborn universe

Led by the Silver River's shadow
Which glistens on
The model Grace's
Amber cheeks

* Silver River is the Milky Way.

74

We set sail
Ride in a canoe
With fifteen unformed brothers of the spirit
Of the universe

It's boundless
It's chaotic
A certain story of the earth that began in spring 1967
Changes from sandals to a ship
Sets out towards the universe
I see a wind of this
In the strict winter of early spring 1976

Already the earthling
Sets sail from a human story starbound
Trying to hugely curve
Thought, hope, and despair
Into Noah's ark

That sense of curving
Never allows the curse toward the 21st century
To stand straight up

The curve magnanimously
Invites, bends down, gets sentimental
And tempts the rudeness of verticality
To its own side

We hear the sound of waves
Hear it very close
So we think it's a propeller's sound
The music the old time space pilots
Were once familiar with

Cutting back time
The sound of waves gradually turns toward earth
On earth
Mankind is innocent yet evil
Slumbering, playing
On the earth's beach where waves roll in
I paddle my canoe
From 1976 to early 1975
Up to my knees in earth's sea
I walk along Manila's shore
Fragrant with warm sunbeams
Offshore no enemy ships
On shore no enemy's armored vehicles
But
More invisible enemies
Than hundreds and millions of Manila mosquitoes
Are spying on me
Preparing assaults of gentle death
For each and every cell of my skin
I walk on Manila's seashore
Bathed in many sunbeams
Seeing in the First Lady's
Marvelous elegant smiles
And in her soldiers' dark expressionless eye sockets
Unimaginable dungeons

Quezon, on a front street in Manila
There's an ancient three storied house
One hundred years old
The woman owner isn't there
She went to the other world long ago
Her husband, a seaman,
Is also now in the sea
For thirty years, even longer, he's been in the sea
His daughter believes
The sea has no graveyard only romance
When she was about seven years old

The island is burning, hell becomes the island
Island becomes hell, hell becomes island
Island becomes hell, between hell and the island
She is playing the piano
The seven-year-old daughter called Virginia
Runs desperately over the keyboard
Among the whites and blacks
Death and scanty hope graze her slightly
Sweaty nose-tip
Trying to catch up with them
She all the more desperately strikes at the keyboard
PEACH
She puts a cooled cold peach with ice
In a cut glass vessel
Fearfully she takes it to the enemy country's officer
Making her large bird eyes larger
Suddenly
The piano sounds stop
The piano vanishes
"Who plays this piano?
I want you to play now"
The man pronounces
Fluently, quietly, in precise English
Yet Virginia the seven-year-old girl
Almost drops to the floor her English
With which to reply to this messenger from hell
Precisely, quietly, fluently
She is holding desperately in her tiny hands
The English that threatens to fall on the floor
And break into pieces
She says: "MAMA ISN'T HOME"

Since that day
On a front street in Quezon, Manila
At the ancient three storied house
One hundred years old this year

There are no piano sounds
Virginia's fingers hit the typewriter
Pronouncing poetry and making dramas in staccato
Like Jeanne d'Arc
Her slender strong fragile fingers
No longer touch the piano

In front of a disco a gunshot rings out
One shot, two shots
Shot by the enemy
(But this time internal enemy
It's the internal enemy with the same Tagalog blood)
Shot by the enemy, the young poet Willie Sanchos
Has blood spurting out his thigh
Willie Sanchos
Appears in America in New York, from time
To time in Manila and in Japan
But this Willie who appears in a Manila disco
Is always a ghost
He is alive
The incident occurred three long years ago
But Willie
Willie's ghost is still wandering
Glued to the front door
Of a Manila disco

Someone drops poetry along with their legs
It's difficult to pick up the muse like fresh bread
From among concrete fragments shattered
Into pieces and blood
In the end
Evening at Fort Santiago the stronghold
The old castle ruins
End of January in Manila's nightsky
Stars shower ceaselessly, it's summer
No, it's a soft spring night

On the stone wall of Fort Santiago
Hundreds and thousands of ancestral spirits
Rise with sunset
While thousands of mosquitoes softly sing a requiem
The sacred lecher
Appears from inside me and makes love with their spirits
Mosquitoes quietly back away

Easter
At resurrection some die
Going against those who revive from death to life
A black haired white necked woman rides
A car towards death
Morality puts a knife in her nerves
But no one looks for the demons
Who put knives in morality

No, the demons who put knives in each other
Sing a lullaby by morality's pillow
But the baby won't stop crying
And morality the wet nurse won't easily
Put a mirror to her own face
Because she has no face
Many countries to hide faces
Are hiding and sleeping
Under the pillow
Under the mattress

Overhead
Easter passes
Easter
Just like a propeller's sound
Carrying many messengers from the universe
Carrying the Buddha, Christ, Titan, Allah the Almighty,
Mohammed, other evil spirits, good spirits, all spirits
As it appears on Easter evening

The earth chokes over spring
Suddenly
Fermenting life chokes
Over the tumult of death
Sliding past these seasons
The propeller sound inside me
In truth is the sound of waves lapping the beaches
Of the universe
Lured by this
I get on a boat
I get in a canoe

A canoe carrying
A youth with beautiful eyes
Said to have escaped from off Manila
Into the universe
Inside me
It comes paddling
Soundlessly

June
In the sky of Rotterdam
Hundreds of orange balloons rise
Accompanied by the sacred lecher
Up in the too blue sky of Holland
This one canoe also appears

Seasons do not refuse the canoe
Space does not refuse the canoe
Canoe has a passport of illusion
Like all of the spirits
And messengers of the universe
Canoe has a passport of illusion
Wet with the waves of spirits
Where silver fish cross-fly

Sound of waves lapping gradually grows fiercer
Louder on the beaches of the universe
On the model Grace's amber cheeks
Silver waves lap the Silver River
There someone is fishing for beauty
A close-up of the face of Grace, the model,
Covers the whole universe
Then her face becomes pitch-dark
Unfathomable abyss
Many invisible black holes
Are waiting inside her face
We can't go inside her dignified and erotic face
We can only wink from earth
Like wind
To her cheeks the Silver River

The traveler appeared; the traveler departed
From the summer of 1975
To the yearend when I was listening
To Earth, Wind, and Fire
The traveler was young, birds are gentle
Continuously cooking delicious music
Placed it on the dish of limited time
While eating it saw one or two movies

>A stray child's soul on roller skates
>Runs to the future world
>Can never return
>Weeps
>We forget to give even one handkerchief

After the movie young travelers
Are laughing, drinking wine
Trying out records one after another
Seeking the sounds for the next course

You can neither shoot
Nor eternally crucify these times
That's why anyone can easily become a traveler
From myself to my other self
From one season in me to another season
In the meantime
The full moon appeared several times
Each time I parted from a young traveler and friends

Alone I open the curtain of thought
Oh, look at the hundreds and thousands of windows
Attached to the doors of the brain—
I open all those windows and doors
Off to the universe inside me
And slide in
In a canoe

I don't know if these can be called the sacred
        lecherous seasons
There's no noise here
Everything is pure erect music
Eros is the sound of water
Eros is beside the wave
Magic is inside the wave
Magic is singing
Magic is eros and beauty

Again the sound of water
Like a propeller's sound
I hear it strongly
From the depths of the universe
Like an incident on earth
Close by I hear it
Coming toward the decaying green earth
And the vomiting sea

These sounds are communications, signals
No Noah's ark
But the ark of the universe
The sound of water, like a propeller's sound
Is splashing water, coming closer
The sounds of greeting

Strict winter, early 1976, three in the afternoon
Standing on a hill in purple misty Musashino
Wearing a Nigerian's mask
I know the person who appears
He's the one who borrowed my form
He's a monk, a Buddha, a traveler like Bashō
Wearing sandals
Who has continued traveling the sacred lecherous seasons
Inside me
He came dropping several lines of poetry
Resembling rice grains
Swiftly that day he disappeared
Into the winter sky of Mitaka
Musashino where UFO's are seen
But the rice grains he dropped are hard
The rice grains he dropped are soft
Whenever we paddle into the sea of thought
We smell rice stalks, we smell soil
Because of the sandals and rice grains he dropped

The seasons of the sacred lecher
Will continue to wander on earth for a little while
Pitch-dark
In the pitch-dark depths of the universe
A silver wave runs, a fish, an electric wave,
A determination runs

Sound of waves gradually coming closer
Here's the Silver River
A hunter is fishing for beauty
At the wave-lapping Silver River
Our guardian deity, the sacred lecher,
Appears and takes a sacred bath
Also a canoe and fifteen unformed brothers
Of the spirit of the universe
Are taking sacred baths beside the Silver River

Boundlessness larger than chaos
Nebulae with much strong energy
Music and will
All become a world turning

Toward a close-up of the model
Grace's amber cheeks
Vertically becoming a comet
Splashing fiercely
It's the traveler who changed from sandals to a canoe
Taking flight
Making the water sound like a propeller

None other than the sacred lecher
And so towards earth and space
In the manner of the two lechers
Butch Cassidy and the Sundance Kid
He becomes shadow and light
Light and shadow
And sets out on a journey

Memo:
March 4th 1976, two o'clock early morning
Crows asleep in the forest of Yoyogi
A comet appears
From Los Angeles, Soul Unlimited's brothers
Play the night's last number in Shinjuku
Joe is composing a new piece

INDEX OF TITLES AND FIRST LINES

DATE DUE	